HOW TO BE A BETTER LEADER
IN
18 DAYS

ISBN: 978-1505646122

Introduction

This 18 day personal development programme is based on selected extracts from Dr Lesley Hunter's Challenge Choice Change (CCC) programme. It is a backed by over a decade of research and brings together three key aspects of effective leader development:

- leader self-awareness
- leader self-regulation
- self-leader behaviour

The CCC framework contains 18 elements of leader behaviour that are grouped into 6 global dimensions. This kick-starter programme has a different element as the focus for each of the 18 days.

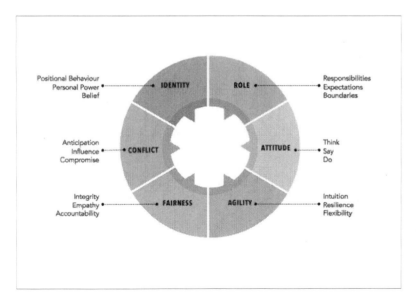

Challenge Choice Change Framework
© Dr Lesley Hunter

How to use this book

Each morning, read the relevant Challenge statements associated with the element for that day. Select the statement that is having the biggest impact on your performance as a leader right now. This may be a negative impact where you need to do something differently or could be a positive impact where you need to consciously focus on doing more of something that is currently working well.

Identify **one thing** you can do for a day that will improve your performance against this statement – keep the activity simple, realistic and manageable.

Keep your focus on that activity throughout the day. Don't try to be too ambitious. You are aiming to interrupt and disrupt your current pattern of behaviour so the individual incremental steps will build into accelerated progress over the period of your 18 day programme.

Each evening, record your thoughts and experiences in the daily journal. Please do not skip this step because this is where you will be able to reflect and identify your key learning.

At the end of the 18 days, take some time to read your daily journal entries and reflect on the changes you have made. Remember that you must hold yourself to account and be honest with yourself.

The 18 day programme will kick-start your development but sustaining behavioural change takes time … it will not happen overnight.

Before you start

Choose your time period carefully – you have to be able to commit to 18 days, although not necessarily 18 consecutive days.

It is very easy to start something with the best intentions but the most difficult part of any development programme is maintaining motivation and seeing it through to completion.

It is inevitable that your focus will waver at some stage during the programme. When it does, come back to this page and pick the affirmation that will motivate you to continue … or write your own in the blank spaces below.

Get a grip!

Slowly but surely - one day at a time

I can do this - I will do this

I have everything I need to succeed

I am learning something new every day

IDENTITY

Positional Behaviour

Positional Behaviour is focused on your ability to recognise and accept your internal state of mind leading to the capacity to exert power on your own emotions and actions. It is not about holding power over another person or influencing or manipulating externally.

Challenge

a) I have a clear frame of reference for my position as a leader.
b) I have a clear understanding of how to behave as a leader.
c) I create strong psychological contracts with my followers.

Choice

Which of the statements above is the one that is having the biggest impact on your performance as a leader right now?

Change

What **one thing** will you do today that will begin to improve your performance against this statement?

_____

Day 1 Journal: Positional Behaviour

_____

_____

_____

_____

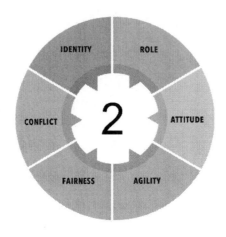

IDENTITY

Personal Power

Personal Power is focused on your own perception and identity as a leader, and your subsequent ability to motivate, influence and guide others' actions. It is not about your status, job title or the degree of authority you are perceived to exert in an organisational hierarchy or structure.

a) I have the personal power to motivate myself.
b) I can control and influence the outcomes of my decisions and actions.
c) I have the personal power to choose how I feel and respond in any given situation.

Which of the statements above is the one that is having the biggest impact on your performance as a leader right now?

What **one thing** will you do today that will begin to improve your performance against this statement?

_____

Day 2 Journal: Personal Power

_____

_____

_____

_____

IDENTITY

Belief

Belief is focused on your own perception and identity as a leader, and your subsequent ability to motivate, influence and guide others' actions. It is not about your status, job title or the degree of authority you are perceived to exert in an organisational hierarchy or structure.

a) I believe in myself and "see" myself as a leader.
b) I believe in what I am trying to achieve.
c) I have confidence in my abilities as a leader.

Which of the statements above is the one that is having the biggest impact on your performance as a leader right now?

What **one thing** will you do today that will begin to improve your performance against this statement?

_____

Day 3 Journal: Belief

_____

_____

_____

_____

ROLE

Responsibilities

Responsibilities is focused on your understanding of the purpose, function and roles of both yourself (as a leader) and the followers in your team, along with the tasks and contribution expected of each team member.

a) I understand the tasks that are required to achieve the outcome I want.
b) I understand the role of my team in relation to the organisation as a whole.
c) I can articulate the responsibilities of each individual member of my team.

Which of the statements above is the one that is having the biggest impact on your performance as a leader right now?

What **one thing** will you do today that will begin to improve your performance against this statement?

_____

Day 4 Journal: Responsibilities

_____

_____

_____

_____

ROLE

Expectations

Expectations is focused on the expectations associated with different roles: your own (as a leader) and also the individuals within your team. Expectations can be defined in terms of behaviour and outcomes and can be measured as performance in each of these areas.

a) I can define and articulate my expectations of each individual member of my team.
b) My expectations are clearly defined as targets and/or objectives.
c) I measure the performance of others in relation to the expectations of their role.

Which of the statements above is the one that is having the biggest impact on your performance as a leader right now?

What **one thing** will you do today that will begin to improve your performance against this statement?

_____

Day 5 Journal: Expectations

_____

_____

_____

_____

Challenge

Choise

Change

ROLE

Boundaries

Boundaries is focused on your understanding of the boundaries of different roles in relation to tasks, leading and developing others, as well as the emotional boundaries you will experience as a leader. Boundaries define the threshold between one individual's "space" and another.

a) I understand the boundaries of my own role as a leader.
b) I can clearly define the boundaries of each individual's role within my team.
c) I accept that my boundaries are not barriers or restrictions that prevent me contributing as a leader.

Which of the statements above is the one that is having the biggest impact on your performance as a leader right now?

What **one thing** will you do today that will begin to improve your performance against this statement?

_____

Day 6 Journal: Boundaries

_____

_____

_____

_____

ATTITUDE

Think

Think relates to your thought processes and decision-making strategies, including the use of visualisation, creative thinking and mental agility. The most effective leaders are self-aware and consequently understand how their thinking processes affect their behaviour and performance.

a) I think creatively when faced with unfamiliar challenges and situations.
b) I use visualisation to create a mental image and "see" what I am trying to achieve.
c) I recognise the importance of understanding "why" when making decisions and taking action.

Which of the statements above is the one that is having the biggest impact on your performance as a leader right now?

What **one thing** will you do today that will begin to improve your performance against this statement?

_____

Day 7 Journal: Think

_____

_____

_____

_____

Challenge

Choice

Change

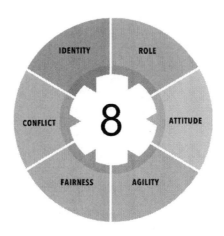

ATTITUDE

Say

Challenge

Say relates to the way you communicate your thoughts and feelings and takes account of the tone, style, consistency and clarity of your approach (verbally and non-verbally).

a) I communicate my thoughts clearly and concisely.
b) I recognise and use a range of delivery styles to ensure my approach is appropriate for the audience.
c) I say what I mean and mean what I say.

Choice

Which of the statements above is the one that is having the biggest impact on your performance as a leader right now?

Change

What **one thing** will you do today that will begin to improve your performance against this statement?

_____

Day 8 Journal: Say

_____

_____

_____

_____

ATTITUDE

Do

Do is the action-oriented element of attitude. A leader is often judged by their actions, i.e. what they do and how they do it.

Challenge

a) I behave in a fair and consistent manner.
b) I create space for innovation and creativity to happen.
c) I am comfortable using emotional displays to increase my effectiveness as a leader.

Choice

Which of the statements above is the one that is having the biggest impact on your performance as a leader right now?

Change

What **one thing** will you do today that will begin to improve your performance against this statement?

_____

Day 9 Journal: Do

_____

_____

_____

_____

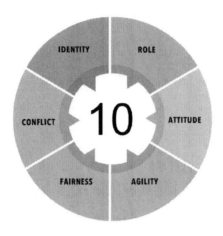

IDENTITY ROLE

CONFLICT **10** ATTITUDE

FAIRNESS AGILITY

AGILITY

Intuition

Intuition is focused on your ability to recognise patterns, understand your own strengths and weaknesses and be able to balance logic and intuitive decision-making. Effective leaders can distinguish between instinct, which is a hardwired autonomous reflex action, and intuition (i.e. feeling of knowing or tip of the tongue phenomenon).

a) I balance an intuitive approach with logical argument.
b) I know when something is right.
c) I recognise patterns linked to my intuitive decision-making.

Which of the statements above is the one that is having the biggest impact on your performance as a leader right now?

What **one thing** will you do today that will begin to improve your performance against this statement?

_____

Day 10 Journal: Intuition

_____

_____

_____

_____

Challenge

Choise

Change

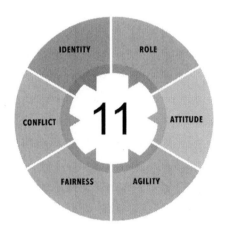

AGILITY

Resilience

Challenge

Resilience is focused on your ability to learn from experiences, including mistakes, and to handle stressful and difficult situations. It links to how you manage and regulate your own emotional state in order to maintain your personal and professional well-being.

a) I am not afraid of experiencing failure.
b) I bounce back from disappointment by reframing the situation and using it as a learning opportunity.
c) I manage my own emotional state effectively.

Choice

Which of the statements above is the one that is having the biggest impact on your performance as a leader right now?

Change

What **one thing** will you do today that will begin to improve your performance against this statement?

_____

Day 11 Journal: Resilience

_____

_____

_____

_____

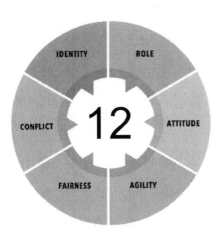

AGILITY

Flexibility

Flexibility is focused on your ability to handle uncertainty and ambiguity. It is about having strategies to cope and adapt in unfamiliar situations and being able to handle and embrace change. Leaders need to demonstrate flexibility at various levels – cognitive, behavioural and emotional.

a) I have developed appropriate strategies to handle uncertainty and ambiguity.
b) I embrace change.
c) I am prepared to seek out innovative and new solutions.

Challenge

Which of the statements above is the one that is having the biggest impact on your performance as a leader right now?

Choice

What **one thing** will you do today that will begin to improve your performance against this statement?

Change

_____

Day 12 Journal: Flexibility

_____

_____

_____

_____

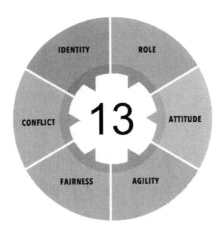

FAIRNESS

Integrity

Integrity is focused on the way in which you treat people. It is associated with dignity, respect, honesty, visibility and developing trust. Integrity is an essential ingredient for a leader to be effective.

a) I behave in an open and transparent manner.
b) I have a strong moral code that underpins my behaviour as a leader.
c) My actions are consistent with both my personal values and the organisational values.

Which of the statements above is the one that is having the biggest impact on your performance as a leader right now?

What **one thing** will you do today that will begin to improve your performance against this statement?

_____

Day 13 Journal: Integrity

_____

_____

_____

_____

FAIRNESS

Empathy

Empathy is focused on how you develop relationships and shared understanding with others. It is also about the development of psychological contracts with followers.

a) I build meaningful and appropriate relationships with my followers.
b) I do not confuse empathy with sympathy.
c) I have a good understanding of the impact I have on others.

Which of the statements above is the one that is having the biggest impact on your performance as a leader right now?

What **one thing** will you do today that will begin to improve your performance against this statement?

_____

Day 14 Journal: Empathy

_____

_____

_____

_____

FAIRNESS

Accountability

Accountability is about holding yourself, and others "to account" for the commitments you are expected to fulfil. It is focused on understanding the impact of your actions as a leader and taking responsibility for the outcomes, but is also about holding others accountable for their contribution as followers.

a) I regularly reflect on my own performance and hold myself accountable for the outcomes.
b) I accept credit and recognition for successes.
c) I understand the impact of my actions.

Which of the statements above is the one that is having the biggest impact on your performance as a leader right now?

What **one thing** will you do today that will begin to improve your performance against this statement?

_____

Day 15 Journal: Accountability

_____

_____

_____

_____

Challenge

Choice

Change

CONFLICT

Anticipation

Anticipation is focused on scanning, assessing and being alert to changing conditions and potential opportunities for conflict. It is also about developing strategies to recognise situations and support decision-making.

a) I am alert to factors and issues that could influence or de-stabilise my team.
b) I can detect emerging conflict in its earliest stages.
c) I recognise the signs and symptoms when conflict could arise.

Which of the statements above is the one that is having the biggest impact on your performance as a leader right now?

What **one thing** will you do today that will begin to improve your performance against this statement?

_____

Day 16 Journal: Anticipation

_____

_____

_____

_____

Challenge

Choice

Change

CONFLICT

Influence

Influence is the capacity to change or affect someone or something and is focused on building networks, communities and alliances to reach collaborative decisions and outcomes. Effective leaders are influence agents who use a range of tactics to influence different targets, depending on the situation at the time.

a) I can influence others to reach collaborative decisions and outcomes.
b) I can influence opinionated people.
c) I have a clear understanding of the difference between influence and persuasion.

Which of the statements above is the one that is having the biggest impact on your performance as a leader right now?

What **one thing** will you do today that will begin to improve your performance against this statement?

_____

Day 17 Journal: Influence

_____

_____

_____

_____

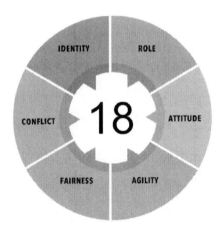

CONFLICT

Compromise

Challenge

Compromise is focused on your ability to see others' points of view and take appropriate action to achieve required outcomes. It also considers your capacity to handle different forms of conflict (task, inter-personal, emotional) and to resolve disputes.

a) I know when it would be appropriate to compromise and when this would not be the right course of action.
b) I can resolve disputes within my team.
c) I stimulate and manage productive conflict.

Choice

Which of the statements above is the one that is having the biggest impact on your performance as a leader right now?

Change

What **one thing** will you do today that will begin to improve your performance against this statement?

_____

Day 18 Journal: Compromise

_____

_____

_____

_____

Next steps

Think of your ongoing leader development as a fitness regime that requires conscious effort and is very similar to building and flexing your muscles.

The full CCC programme combines an online diagnostic (challenge) with an 8-week customised development programme (choice) underpinned by over 100 techniques drawn from coaching, neuro-science and psychology. The final stage (change) involves a signature behavioural modelling strategy that integrates and embeds behavioural change.

Challenge muscles encourage your self-awareness measured against a research based framework of leader behaviour.

Choice muscles present a series of techniques, specifically aligned to your unique profile, to open up options and develop flexibility in your behaviour.

Change muscles are underpinned by a unique elite leader modelling strategy to integrate and embed change in your behavioural repertoire.

Take the next step to continue your leader development journey by joining the full CCC programme and working with Dr Lesley to become an elite leader.

www.challengechoicechange.com

Dr Lesley Hunter

Lesley has achieved a rare balance of practical experience and academic credibility for her work with aspiring and elite leaders.

Lesley's early career in education laid the foundation for her no-nonsense down to earth style of delivery and her ability to analyse and forensically target areas for improvement through extensive experience as a lead inspector of schools in the UK.

Her work in education has transcended international and sector boundaries, from working with school principals and senior leaders in the UK, Europe and throughout the Middle East to delivering leadership development and innovation modules on MBA and MSc programmes for universities in the UK, Hong Kong, Singapore, United Arab Emirates and Geneva.

Lesley has a strong pedigree outside education and has worked in a consultancy capacity with senior leaders in public, private and voluntary sector organisations. She has an unrivalled depth of knowledge and experience in what makes leaders effective and how they can impact on the performance of any organisation.

Her research has explored the need for clear distinctions between 'leadership' and 'leaders' and has led to the creation of the revolutionary Challenge Choice Change construct. Through this work, she has established a wide reach with clients in police forces, military, healthcare and global manufacturing companies, among many others.

If you want some typical traditional **leadership development** then Lesley is definitely not the right person for you.

But … when you are ready to:

- explore how elite leaders think and behave
- look at your own behaviour and how this impacts on the people around you
- consider the dynamics of your team
- improve your own performance and the outcomes you achieve
- invest in your own development and make the transition to being an elite leader

  … then you have found the right person to work with.

Please leave a comment about your progress on this 18 day programme, find out more about Lesley's work and watch her TEDx talk at:

www.lesleyhunter.com

Challenge | Choice | Change

Printed in Great Britain
by Amazon